The AQUARIUM

by Lynne Anderson

Come on! We are going to the aquarium. We are going to see many sea animals.

You can help us count them!

We have to buy tickets before we can see the animals. One ticket costs $5.00. We will buy three tickets. How much will three tickets cost?

$5.00 + $5.00 + $5.00 = $15.00

We see the rays and sharks first.
We see two rays and four sharks.
How many do we see in all?

2 + 4 = 6

Next we see some pretty fish.
We see two yellow fish
and three orange fish.
How many more orange
than yellow fish do we see?

3 − 2 = 1

Then we see one very big octopus and five pretty jellyfish.

How many do we see in all?

1 + 5 = 6

We see the sea horses next.
We see one black sea horse.

We see two light sea horses.
How many more light than
black sea horses do we see?

2 − 1 = 1

Then we see a show. We see three whales jump in the air.

We see a dolphin swim with her baby, too.
How many sea animals do we see in the show?

3 + 2 = 5

The show is over. It is time to go. We can't wait to see the sea animals again!

dolphin

sea horse

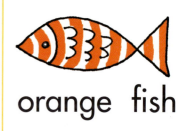
orange fish

jellyfish

octopus

shark

whale

yellow fish

ray